Praise for

Running Toward Water

poems by

Jenna Wysong Filbrun

"In her haunting and lyrical new poetry collection, *Running Toward Water*, Jenna Wysong Filbrun deftly maps the raw terrain of grief, chronic illness, and climate change. Filbrun carries us with her as she goes through the fires of ordinary life and becomes transformed by the one constant she can count on—the power and hope offered in the natural world. These poems are beautifully bound by threads of a spiritual journey. In the end, the poet's well-crafted, musical, and often surprising turns-of-phrase combine to invite us to understand that our humanity cannot be separated from its home and that often the solace we are looking for is right in front of us."

ELLIS ELLIOTT
author of *Break in the Field*, a poetry collection;
and *A Witch Awakens: A Fire Circle Mystery*

✦

"Jenna Wysong Filbrun is one of those special poets who has found that secret nexus of wilderness and sacredness. Like Mary Oliver, she urges us to look around, dig our fingers into loam, and follow wild water to the undomesticated revelation that we may already be in Paradise, such as when she writes, 'I believe / in a place / I can't quite / get to / somewhere / I already / am.' And when I read her poetry, I know it to be true."

NICHOLAS TRANDAHL
award-winning poet, author of *Purgatory* and *Cabin Sketches*

"Jenna Wysong Filbrun's *Running Toward Water* is a stunningly beautiful collection. Drawing intensely on the wide sweep and intricate details of the natural world, it is also personal, lyrical, profoundly human. Filbrun explores memory and the cycles of time, the beauty and fragility of life, and our inevitable encounters with love, pain, and loss. Throughout, her poetry is shot through with slender rays of hope and faith, rays that indicate a still greater light underpinning all our beliefs and all our art. Individual poems show us how to 'breathe and decipher' ('Air Quality Warning') life's ordinary as well as its ultimate mysteries, encourage us to 'hallow the bones as they hollow' ('My Loves, the Earth, My Bones'), and teach us how, in simply and attentively being, we can attain a state of prayer."

SARAH LAW
editor of *Amethyst Review*,
author of *This Transfigured Chapel of the Threads*

✦

"Jenna Wysong Filbrun's poems speak to us from a voice that notices every detail, questions its surroundings, and ultimately, calls out to be heard. In the poem 'On Not Becoming Bitter,' she writes, 'What you think you see is only the shadow / of something more.' In this collection, Filbrun pursues the 'something more' that lies beyond the shadows, and she offers her findings with extraordinary care. 'I want to soften like a seed / in the earth, twine like a root / in the ground, reach like a vine,' she writes in 'Instruction on Lasting.' These poems come from the earth, sprout up, and climb toward the light."

AARON LELITO
editor-in-chief of *Wild Roof Journal*

Running Toward Water

poems by
Jenna Wysong Filbrun

SHANTI ARTS PUBLISHING
BRUNSWICK, MAINE

Running Toward Water

Published by Shanti Arts LLC

Designed by Shanti Arts Designs

Shanti Arts LLC
193 Hillside Road
Brunswick, Maine 04011

shantiarts.com

Cover image is by the author and used with her permission.

Printed in the United States of America

ISBN: 978-1-962082-92-1 (softcover)

LCCN: 2026930453

for Mike,
Oliver, and Lewis

Contents

Acknowledgments _____ 11

Part 1 — Clutch

How the Maple Tree Grandpa Planted by the Barn
    Cracks Open in a Too-Early, Too-Heavy Snow _____ 18

My Loves, the Earth, My Bones _____ 19

Air Quality Warning _____ 20

Our Violence _____ 21

Like a Bedside Vigil _____ 23

Intact _____ 24

Dead Weight? _____ 25

Clutch _____ 26

Missing the Trees for the Forest _____ 27

On Epistemology _____ 28

Sometimes I Fall _____ 29

Mild Winter, Early Spring _____ 30

What to Trust _____ 31

[All summer I wait] _____ 32

August _____ 33

On Not Becoming Bitter _____ 34

Part 2 — Immersion

Ash Wednesday: A Recognition _____ 38

Edna Spurgeon Acres Land Trust, April _____ 39

Pileated Woodpeckers _____ 40

Pain and Wellness _____ 41

Spring Peepers _____ 42

How We Get Through This _____ 43

Patio _____ 44

Cabin Porch _____ 45

Pack Animal _____ 47

Eleven Mile Canyon _____ 48

"Little Incident" _____ 49

Us _____ 50

Clarity _____ 51

Mirrors _____ 52

Much More than Divine Intervention _____ 53

Larger Than the Happenings of Days _____ 54

Ask Grief _____ 55

The Holy Hours _____ 57

How a Spirit Leaves a Body *(Remember?)* _____ 58

Like It Was _____ 59

Immersion _____ 60

Why Try to Put Words to It (Ars Poetica) _____ 61

Part 3 — Offering

Instruction on Lasting _____ 64

Sassafras _____ 65

Only Silence _____ 66

Western Tanager _____ 67

Lost Creek Wilderness (Communion) _____ 68

First, the Daffodils _____ 69

Daylilies _____ 70

Illness _____ 71

Be-ing _____ 72

Burning Bush *(Euonymus Alatus)* _____ 73

Photograph on the Landing _____ 74

Offering _____ 75

Clearing Branches _____ 77

Mo[u]rning _____ 78

For Courage _____ 79

Forgiveness _____ 80

Spirit Spiriting (Second Dog) _____ 81

Stream over the Trail _____ 82

A Geode in a Dream _____ 83

To Time _____ 84

Living and Dying _____ 86

In Harmony _____ 87

Gloria Patri in Snowflakes _____ 88

I Try to Lay the Prayer of My Life on the House
    of What Lasts _____ 89

Notes _____ 93

Additional Thanks _____ 95

Acknowledgments

The author extends her gratitude to the editors of the following publications in which these poems first appeared, often in slightly different form:

Amethyst Review: "Sometimes I Fall" and "To Time"

Autumn Sky Poetry Daily: "Burning Bush (*Euonymus Alatus*)"

Blue Heron Review: "I Try to Lay the Prayer of My Life on the House of What Lasts" and "Mirrors" (Best of the Net and Pushcart Prize Nominee)

Crosswinds Poetry Journal: "Only Silence"

Deep Wild Journal: "Western Tanager" and "Little Incident"

The Dewdrop: "Lost Creek Wilderness (Communion)" (Pushcart Prize Nominee)

EcoTheo Review: "How the Maple Tree Grandpa Planted by the Barn Cracks Open in a Too-Early, Too-Heavy Snow"

Gyroscope Review: "Immersion"

ONE ART: a journal of poetry: "Illness"; "Like It Was"; "My Loves, the Earth, My Bones"; and "On Not Becoming Bitter"

Snapdragon: A Journal of Art & Healing: "How We Get Through This"

Thin Places & Sacred Spaces, Amethyst Press (anthology): "A Geode in a Dream"

Tiny Seed Literary Journal: "First, the Daffodils" and "Why Try to Put Words to It (Ars Poetica)"

The Half-Life of Echoes, tiny wren lit (anthology): "Intact"

Unearthed Journal: "Ask Grief" and "For Courage"

The Way Back to Ourselves: "Dead Weight?"; "Instruction on Lasting"; and "Pileated Woodpeckers"

Wild Roof Journal: "Our Violence"

Most of the following poems were written within the ancestral homelands of the Bodéwadmi/Potawatomi and Myaamia/Miami peoples (also known as Northern Indiana) and the Ute people (Central Colorado). Due to colonization, broken treaties, and forced removals, many members of these Indigenous communities remain separated from these sacred lands that their people have cared for over hundreds of years.

There is only one prayer left:
"Teach us to pray."
Teach us to pray.

—Annie Dillard

—*Part 1*—

Clutch

How the Maple Tree Grandpa Planted by the Barn Cracks Open in a Too-Early, Too-Heavy Snow

As the light turns yellow, then gray, then yellow.
As the wind blows still-green leaves from the trees.
As the dogs drape and sigh on the curl of my legs
against the unusual hues.
As rain, then sleet falls in waving sheets
that clump to streams of snow.

In a slow arc of pop and crash.
With a bounce that swipes the white clumps
from the green-orange-tipped, full-fingered leaves.
Onto the still shock
of the grassy, snow-caked ground.

As I watch from the window with arms
that can't stop it, heart flopping.

My Loves, the Earth, My Bones

after osteoporosis at 33

Sometimes finitude screams in my head.
I try to let it be like I try to wear with serenity
the fact that my bones are hollowing.
But there is a desperate edge to the miles.
As if I could hallow the bones as they hollow—
fill them with enough mountaintop,
enough deep woods to last
past when they're too gone to take me there.

I am not talking only of bones.
I want to hear how the good things last
if what holds us up
can't outlast us.

That's what I think as I traipse down
the mountain in the rain
or wake up panicked in the night.
I go deeper into the mists of love
I need like thunder to see
even as I cling to a horse
in a dream, galloping
through the dark
with no reins.

Air Quality Warning

The sun oranges its way
through the far-off, gray sky.
The wind brings the vaporized
Canadian trees to cling
to our damp, heavy air.
Our trees breathe and decipher.
What are fine particulates of pine
to a maple, a honey locust?
Do the cottonwoods recognize
their cousins in the haze?
I spend the days indoors,
windows down.
I turn out the light
on the thick nights
and dream about fire.
I run through a mansion
as it breaks out in flame.
In one untouched wing, room
after calm, wood-trimmed room
is covered with lit candles.
I dash from flame to flame,
trying to put them all out.

Our Violence

When joy
brittles

like a leaf
or a bone

it becomes something
to release

and to tend.
It is ok

to get heartsick over all
our death.

Love runs with
suffering

never in spite of it.
It is winter now.

Where the bare trees
merge and feather,

a light glimmers
between the trunks—

the sun
in the far-off creek water.

At night,
the owl calls

from the bone-white
branches of the sycamore

behind the barn.
Joy is somewhere

in the folds of his voice
as it ripples

through the empty limbs
in reach of the moon.

Like the next heartbeat.
And the next.

Like a Bedside Vigil

We wait for the solar eclipse, for the moon
to turn down the dial of red spring trees and bright green grass
toward mid-day darkness.

Last year's sycamore leaves
scrape across the pavement
like figure skaters.

Maroon tree-tips wave
where brown and white trunks sway
in slow dance to the pollen song.

It has all the words
you'd expect like *falling*
and *carried away*.

But it begins in the roots
where the old leaves' old leaves
crumble in darkness.

Or whatever it is
that exists
between light.

Intact

The stories
she used to tell
survive—
When the swamp freezes,
I think about the time
she slipped through
a crack in the ice
in her skates, age nine.
Her memory.
Still on the surface.

Dead Weight?

Where the prayers were
is an emptiness that swallows.
Under that, a fire.
Then a heavy stone

I carry everywhere.
Ascending the mountain,
hummingbirds zing
at the stone's flame-red hue

the way they hover
before each fiery fold
of the paintbrush petals
to drink.

The red-orange flower blooms
among the rocks on the hill
and does not need to feel anything
to know what is true.

Clutch

I can say what I need to say
about the way the world
cracks apart

to the robin chicks
in the nest on the downspout
over the course of an early spring.

I tell them I'm uncertain now
of everything. They open
the dark drops of their eyes.

I tell them I have no peace.
They poke their beaks from the edge
like points in a woven crown.

I tell them my heart is on fire.
They bob and shift in the nest
like flame.

When they leave, it is sudden
and entire. There then lies
the empty bowl.

The brush and whoosh of wings
the first fruits
of desire.

Missing the Trees for the Forest

When loneliness swells, you get an ache
in your stomach that spreads through your chest.
You dream of alpine meadow trails beyond
you trapped in a room of block walls.
Your spirit is the one horse left behind
thrashing full speed around the fences.

You overlook the sun on the yellow-green
ridges of the just-opening leaves.
You miss the pearl-white petals
that bloom from the red bloodroots.
You neglect the essence of sycamore seeds
that open to scatter with the wind.

So you have to let loneliness fly.
Because if you try to control your desire
for control, isn't that still control?
Look how the little violets
that pepper the grass with purple
seem simply glad to be blooming.

On Epistemology

There is a detour down our road, and now, all day the cars
whoosh and fade past the field at the edge of the woods
we are letting go back to forest.
It is mostly walnut starts so far, their fronds
of waving leaves strewn through the grass. Walnuts
always make me think how G. used to say they knew
which kids in class were the poorest
because their fingers were walnut-stained in the fall.
And how everyone had a crush on this one boy,
Eugene, because he was so clean.

Yesterday, a turtle buried her eggs
in the flower garden next to the snapdragons,
then made her way back toward the swamp
with her slow plod of peel and plant.
The skin on her hind legs stretched and wrinkled
like crinkled paper with each high-stepping stride
down the drive toward the road, and the cars
coming fast.

I wonder what will happen to the field when we're gone.
I mean someday, will it just be the snapping turtles
climbing over crumbling trash (new every morning
like the dew, like manna in reverse)
under the walnut trees, back into the swamp?
And is that hope?

In a few months, I will watch
for the hatchlings, to help them cross the road,
the way M. helped their mother.
I want to see how they know
to dig out of the ground
and totter their holy
little legs toward water.

Sometimes I Fall

through
the notes
of a song

like light
through
a window

at this
bright peace
and thirst

this
alive
and fragile

cruel
and
deep

beauty
so good
I believe

in a place
I can't quite
get to

somewhere
I already
am

Mild Winter, Early Spring

March,
and a snapping turtle hatchling
crawls through the just-green grass.

A new bit of wrinkled-white
eggshell lines the mouth
of the nest

where the others dug out
from the garden
last September.

A miracle? An omen?
Even if I try to pray these days,
there are too many omens

for authentic *Amens*.
Near on the page but far in the mouth,
omen's tensed lips

are closer to the truth
than *Amen's*
open-jaw surrender.

In April, the tulips
come up too early,
all different colors.

Instead of the last spritz of snow
from the sky, mosquitoes
swarm up from the ground.

What to Trust

Turkey Run State Park, Indiana, Spring

I keep coming to the end of myself.
  I begin to run the way water
    runs for the river.

The way it slides and drips
  through rock, rushes
    from limestone ledge.

The way it tumbles downstream
  toward twisting light.
    At nightfall, the light

moves into the water. It runs blue,
  then gold, then pale yellow.
    It chimes as it drips

in the cavern. It trickles and gurgles
  past limb and stone to slip
    into the river.

[All summer I wait]

All summer I wait
for the ironweed to bloom
so the butterflies will come
flex their church window wings
on the purple tufts.

The first monarch arrives late
and alone, drop-skipping
over the field like nothing
has changed but herself,
which is enough.

August

The last lily opens on the stem,
and that rich yellow
is the whole luscious summer.

The flower has its day, then folds
with an elegant drape
to a muted shrivel.

I clip the woody stems
from where they stand
in the leaves like bones.

On Not Becoming Bitter

Someone is sending you a message.
It says maybe we could be friends.

It says you do not have to bow to the gods
of What People Think and What People Say.

Remember how the ruby-throated hummingbird
hung in the air to look you in the eye, and

wasn't it just yesterday you were out
combing the maples for the owl

you thought you heard, whose hoots
rippled from deep in the leaves like a murmur?

If you let the questions unspool,
they will carry you down

their sparkling trails toward sleep.
The way through will come to you later.

It says don't give up.
If it hurts, it is love.

What you think you see is only the shadow
of something more.

What you know
is a gift I would like to open.

It says things
come apart.

You have to let them
come apart.

—Part 2—

Immersion

Ash Wednesday: A Recognition

From the corner of my eye
a light mass

with outstretched legs
streaks through the evergreen trees.

I run my eyes over every limb,
every break in the needles.

Through one slim slot
I spot the stern hook of beak

below black marble eyes
in a creamy, round face.

He watches me look for him
until the gleam of fiery dust in me

peers back from its own
perch in the boughs.

Owl to owl
and branches to branches.

Edna Spurgeon Acres Land Trust, April

All I really need to know about myself
is when I step up and down the hills
over the forest floor in the silent
purple-white uproar of phlox
and trillium in full bloom, my lungs
do only a bit of the breathing.

As sun streams through the weave
of young leaves in the spidery trees,
I am one with this goodness
as certain as each limp lump of leaf
on each twig-entwined branch
is certain of its rust-green glow.

Pileated Woodpeckers

Brown grass half-buried
in white cloud.
Moon slinking through sky
inching toward blue.
Tree tips just turning
orange and red, still
as dancers on stage
before the music starts.

A shrill rattle erupts
eerie over the fog,
like the deep clench
of loneliness
spoken out loud.
And listen.
Across the field,
loneliness answers.

Pain and Wellness

Pain is the liquid
        I swig in a dream

and can't swallow
           and can't

      spit out.
So I live

           with it there
     in my cheeks

taking up
        my mouth.

In the morning, *the leaves*,
you say with soft eyes,

are poking out of the buds
on the maple tree.

The dogs sprawl
over my form in the covers.

The sparrows fly in and out
of the slits in the barn

with bits of grass
in their beaks.

Spring Peepers

When the days ache
like teeth, I sleep
the sleep of trains
running off the rails.

I collect the teeth
that crumble
from my mouth.

I wake with a start
to the tumble
and smother
of darkness.

At last, the sun
crawls down
the trees.

A few frogs croak
from near the creek
to speak earthy warmth
into budding branches.

You can forgive yourself.
You can keep your teeth.
You can forget about time.

How We Get Through This

Red welts
bloom over my body
in slow succession
after weeks of sickness.
I scramble from closed door
to closed door all day on the phone
until control shudders away
in a pathetic pile of limbs on the floor.
Your hand swirls a small circle
on my back from which love
comes curling out the hard shell of me
to feel again through the red
the rich earth in its tendrils.

Patio

Our clean, wet dogs stretch
over the warm, dusty bricks,
gnaw at the sticks within reach,
and pause to sniff the wind.

Pollen puffs from the pines
toward the amber and citrine bodies
of two orioles and three goldfinches
in the branches of the silver maples.

Bees buzz around the railroad ties
that line the edge of the bricks.
The robin watches from her nest
on the downspout.

We lean back in the gray stack chairs,
here to touch the hem of summer
as it passes. And there is healing in it—
the abundance of this one little square.

Cabin Porch

for M.

I will always remember
how we sat on this swing
in the mornings.

The hot coffee
in the crisp air was the sweet
steam of waking.

The world was light
like the tweets from the pines,
steady like the breeze
in the boughs.

The air was sage
fresh, dew moistened,
sweet pine swept.

The light was strong
and insistent, turning
the dewdrops that hung
from the awning
to amethysts.

It was just us
and the mornings,
which felt like the miles,
the peaks, the valleys,
the sun on the rocks,
the coyote trotting
through the meadow,
the mule deer fawn
springing across the trail,

the small birds
landing in the near branches
to cock their heads
and chirp at us, to ask,
Well?

Pack Animal

We drove over the country without them,
and now I'm stuck
in the deep, round concavity

where those little dogs
should be.

Eleven Mile Canyon

How many times was I here as a child
on a rock in the sweet wind, away from all
but the people who loved me, the deep blue sky,
the granite boulders, and the white water
calling me to its clear, shallow pools?

Twenty years later, I am back with you
between the red rock walls
of picnics and laughter,
soft words and small toes
curled in cold, rushing water.

Voices weave with the river static
like the current sparkles through the lattice
of willow branch shadows
to gush white around boulders
still watching over the riverbed.

When we climb back up the bank,
I feel certain they will be there,
packing away potato chips
and pecan shortbread cookies, smiling
as they fold the yellow tablecloth.

A family of merganser ducks
swims upstream where we sit
with our feet in the water. The ducklings
pile on their mother's back
to ride her wake up the rapids.

"Little Incident"

When I thought I lost you
over the rocks on the summit, I turned my body
inside out. I wore my mind like skin
so thinking could be my largest organ.
I shrank my heart to quarter-size
and shoved it on the shelves of my ribs.
I let my lungs go,
and the wind took them away.

When seconds-hours later
I found you ok, the tectonic plates
of me crashed back together.
My mind contracted to retreat
to my skull. My heart exploded
from my ribs. My lungs heaved
their way back into my body.

Now there is a range of peaks
where a soft sea lay before.
What was at the bottom
is up in the light
in all its glory
and terror.

Us

More than anything, we are
the sun on the rocks
and raspberry blooms—
white petals on pink/gray glitter.
Blue peaks unroll far past the horizon
like time laid out to see.
It cannot be an accident. This
existence. The way we hover
together on this mountain
with what's between us—
both ancient rock and new petal,
all the good
that's ever existed
through pain,
bound up with wind
with water
with dust
and light.

Clarity

3:17 a.m.—Turmoil stampedes
around the walls of me.

There is no stopping the hot tingle of panic
when it zig-zags the night hours.

I hear you clear your throat in a way
that means you're awake.

I needle beside you, and you wrap me
in your arms to rub away the knot you know

is always there in the small of my back.
The pounding stops. My breath deepens.

Like at the creek, with you, chaos
breaks apart and slides over the meadow

into the canyon, down the rocks,
leaving only me, knowing.

Mirrors

When I turned to the trees,
they were curious and soft-smiling,
even when I told them I was breaking.
They didn't stiffen with blame,
didn't explain why I was wrong.
They nodded and leaned in to listen.
Yes, they said when I told the whole truth,
You belong here with us.

When I went to the mountains,
the peaks ducked and towered
over the hills. They tucked me
into their folds and told me
how to be alive. How joy
is not something you feel,
but something you become—
these boulders, this butterfly,
these heart-cracks of thunder
that tremble the ground,
this hill rounding
down to the stream.

Now you become
tree-like and mountain-like,
says a nudge
when I try to pray.

Much More than Divine Intervention

Sometimes love presses warm
on my aching head
with its little showings—

A friend appears at the door
with a marked-up manuscript,
hours etched on the pages.

A berry-red cardinal
beams in the brown tree
against the gray sky.

The orchestra of bare trees
welcomes the evening sun,
each playing its own hue of bronze.

The tap of Oliver's heart
presses my lap to the beat
of the crickets on the cool air.

Larger Than the Happenings of Days

After the long, hot hours, we stretch our legs
with the trees in the lowering light.
They buzz with the going on of life
larger than the happenings of days.
The blackberries grow over the rusty gate
and ripen from ruby red to dark purple.
The patch of poison ivy spreads into the grass.
We skirt past to stand under the cottonwoods
and peer high into the shimmering branches.
The air thickens as the wind settles
to a breeze that spirals the pods
on the honey locust. They dangle
like strange ornaments hung
so we will see.

What if it's all
a seed?

Ask Grief

"...having perceived you as [one] who is
'a greater myself'..."
—Teilhard de Chardin

I do learn to free the things
winging into the cage of me.
When the pink morning
makes the orange trees blaze,
there is no saying no
to something that holds
that kind of light.

I stand in the silent bowl
of night ending in flame
and know the endless fire
of a greater myself.

Who can tell
about beginnings
and endings?

About the amount of pain
the world can take
as power-gorged tornadoes
spin around themselves
leaving nothing but bare ground

I tell myself
you can still believe
it all ends
as it begins
in this light.

Ask the earth
about winter
and seeds.

Ask grief
if love
will have the last word.

The Holy Hours

Yes the dawn,
but also the dusk
of an autumn day
when the sky soaks
the last of the sunlight
from the fiery tops
of the still trees,
and darkness spills
to reveal our world
within infinite worlds, spinning.
When I slip through the cracks
of being into a dream
where I am in the backseat
of a car you are driving.
You smile and nod to someone
in the passenger's seat, gesturing
in the ways I know like my own skin
and thought I had forgotten.
You can't hear me
as I call your name, cry out
I miss you, become
desperate. But you flash
that little half smile
over your shoulder,
like you know I am near
as you drive us
through the night
toward wherever it is
we are going.

How a Spirit Leaves a Body *(Remember?)*

The part of the maple that remains
after the split
turns the brightest gold of its life—
nearly luminescent.
I think it must be dying.

Outside with Lewis in the late fall wind,
a southerly gust lifts the leaves
from the shining tree. It blows them
past the splintered center
right at us and away.

For a short time, we swirl
in the cloud of that light.

Like It Was

Yesterday, a finch
flutter-flapped from the barn
like the sound of a horse
clearing his nose.
I could smell the sweet
sweat smell of the horse
coming around the corner.
Hear ripe grass ripping
into crunch and chew,
snort and stomp,
swish swish toss of tail.
Sometimes the old life
passes over this way, smooth
and warm like a neck,
like a velvet nose
lipping my hair.

Immersion

In a cave archaeologists believe
could have been inhabited by John the Baptist,
twenty-eight steps lead from the opening
down to the immersion pool.

The pains of the day
are bedded down
under the covers
and pillows of rest.
The dog lies
with his side
pressed against
the length of me,
pressed against
the length of you,
pressed against
the other dog,
sprawled over
all of us.
I may not be
entirely canine
but I am learning
how to breathe
with the whole,
how to pile
my beating heart
on the warmth
of us, then heave
our sides together
toward sleep.
In other words,
here I am
praying.

Why Try to Put Words to It (Ars Poetica)

Because the door of words
is thick and worn. Each groove is smooth
with touch and weather.

Two cross-bars hold the walnut
planks together, and a push-latch springs
it loose with the *clook* of wood on wood.

Out wells the smell of rain
on winter-bare earth, as full as eyes
meeting across a room.

It slides on its hinge,
the wind of soft music
in low light.

On the other side, wet sage
livens the air in the sun.
Bitter-ripe willows

cover the curve
of the creek where it widens
into the meadow.

An eagle soars by on dark wings.
I cross over into the endless
galaxies of things I don't know

with the desire of water
          running
                    toward water.

—Part 3—

Offering

Instruction on Lasting

When hope only aches in my throat,
it takes me out to pace
among the towering trees
in the tender grass.
The trill of presence
passes through the mouths
of tree frogs and the beaks of birds.
The morning sun carries joy into the day.
The trees reach their stark arms
into the stream of it.
A deer crunches through the brush
in the cloud of her breath.
She steps staccato,
then bounds the field in a flurry of flight.
A dandelion orb glows with frost in the light
to fill the mouth of the finch
who comes to gather its seeds
in a beak bouquet of cotton.

I want to soften like a seed
in the earth, twine like a root
in the ground, reach like a vine,
turn like a leaf, break
into oneness like an old tree.

I want the world
to change
me.

Sassafras

The sassafras tree, according to our guide,
tends to stay small here in the Midwest,
where other trees crowd it out.
It turns the full spectrum of fall colors—
from green to yellow to orange to red.
Its leaves are many-shaped—
the single lobe, the mitten, the raised arms.
People make tea and root beer
from its leaves, roots, and bark
but should drink it in moderation,
now that we know it is carcinogenic.
Once believed to cure all ills,
the tree was exported around the world
prior to the debunking of its magic.

We stop beneath one uniquely tall tree
to marvel at the stained-glass window
of its green-yellow-orange-red light.
It casts its many-shaped shadows
over our heads as we stand in the miracle
of the oneness of its being.

Only Silence

In the dark
by the field,
the huff
of a startled deer
sounds at my side
past the grass.
But no crash
from the crush
of fleeing feet.
Only silence.
It's just me,
I whisper
into the ceiling
of fresh-opened leaves,
darker than the dark
sky and its faint sparkle.
In time, I turn back
toward the house,
the night more alive
even than the day
and the many
preoccupations
I sift through to get to
this moment,
which was always
under all the moments.
The way our ways
cross in the dark.
The way the vast,
unspecified dark
crosses through
our ways.

Western Tanager

The small, yellow-orange sun
of a western tanager
blazes between the branches
of the lodgepole pines.

Don't get me wrong,
we still have our problems.
But as we watch
that little bird

in breathless stillness,
we forget we have bodies
that are not that body,
as he takes wing and alights.

We do not think about
thinking about him
until later,
when we remember.

For a few sacred seconds, we
blaze through the branches.

Lost Creek Wilderness (Communion)

If you come up above the tree line,
        be like the boulders
                balanced on the tundra.
                        Drink the silence
                between the gusts of wind
        that push the clouds
near your fingertips.
        Say a prayer at the altar
                of impossible vastness,
                        of permanence
                                beyond ground and sky.
                                It will take all
                        your breath and strength
                to come up and every resolve
you possess to go back down.
        But do this,
                as often as you do it,
                        to remember.
                                You belong by being.
                        You exist in the memories.
                Only a few of them are yours.
        Here, all the holy ones
                breathe, even
                        the rocks,
                                even
                                    you.

First, the Daffodils

When the snow melts, the rogue daffodils
are first to spike from the brown ground.

They form a line of green at the edge
of the woods, waiting.

The sun shines on the shoots when it can.
It insists, *I am in you.*

In time, mini suns of bright yellow
flowers open and unwither.

They shine full-bodied on the gray meadow
as the other flowers begin to grow.

Soon into the fullness of spring's luster,
the yellow blooms that were all we had

curl and fall, gladly lost
in the now-pervasive glow.

Daylilies

The hibiscus starts we brought
from the old house—mere shoots
we cut from the trunk of the mother shrub
and stuck in the ground—have grown and leafed
beyond their wire enclosures. The deer
have left them alone. Unlike the daylilies
from which the tops have been lopped clean off
the bright yellow buds almost ready to bloom.
But the stubs still open and shine
their dabs of irregular incandescence
from the dusky fronds in the fading light.
Wishing things were different, I imagine,
as they bloom beyond any outcome
or certainty.

Illness

When a windstorm
blasts in from the north
with a sudden
and desperate rage,
even the cottonwoods bow
to the white sheets of rain.

Behind the single
silver-green leaf
plastered to the glass
of the patio door, you can see
the awful flailing
of the trees flying apart
like someone drowning.

When all you can do
is keep your heart
close to the hurt,
you keep it close.

Be-ing

After rain torrents rip through the trees,
water wells over the prairie.
Tree frogs resurrect
the spring song midsummer
to crisscross the flooded field.
Seams of wind skim the water
like the frog trills trail a finger
as they fly back and forth
from under the hooded trees.

You are here?

        I am here.

You are here?

        I am here.

You are here.

        I am here.

Burning Bush *(Euonymus Alatus)*

for O.

I can't hold together
what is bound
to come apart.

Someone I love is dying,
and my whole being flares
like the scarlet blaze

of our bush
against the brown wood
of the barn in November.

The one we grew from a start
off the one at the old house
my husband grew from a start

off the one at his parents' house
their friends gave them
when his grandfather died.

Today the bush is as bright in the sun
as any fire, unconsumed.
Clear as any voice, the red

leaves it will lose
say this dying
is not the end of being.

The love in me, too,
says it's true.
I take off my shoes

in surrender,
desperate to believe
my own fire.

Photograph on the Landing

The water gushed
under the footbridge
in the June snowstorm.
We were the sweet pines,
the three of us,
with our fresh, frozen sap,
and our lacy, fine fingers.
We were the roaring creek
and the steady rocks.
We were the birds
tucked under the boughs
and the chipmunks
huddled underground.

When we turned back,
there were no tracks.

Offering

The neighbor cat
keeps leaving offerings
on the cement by the barn.

I spot the lumps of still bodies
from the house and go out
to bear them to the field.

Today's mouse is brown
with a white snout and whiskers.
Impeccable toes grace too-still feet.

Her eye with no light in it—
not even the quick flash of fright—
is an answer with no question.

I can feel the holiness
of the little mouse—
leaf of leaves, star of stars—

as I carry her to the field
in the curve of the silver trowel.
I wonder where she was going

as she passed through the grass
or under the gap of the door into fear.
Her small being, the throb

of her suffering,
is a connective tissue
through the fissure of time.

Some things matter
the way the laying of flowers
matters more than the flowers

or the lighting of a sacred candle
is the real flame. And isn't that
hope?

Clearing Branches

After the wind roars,
rattles the windows,
creaks the walls,
howls over the roof,

branches lie
beneath the trees in the pasture
like stones
in a cemetery.

The maples are rough and twiggy.
The cottonwoods, knobby and curved.
The long limbs of the sycamores
are solid and smooth, like bones.

It takes legs to lift the branches.
Quickened breath to carry them to the edge
of the woods where they will lie
long past all of us.

To collect treetops in my arms
is a kind of seeing.
Each piece of gnarled bark in my hands
another prayer.

Mo[u]rning

with a line from Cristina M.R. Norcross

Nothing will stay in my hands.
The dogs' water sloshes onto my slippers.
The phone clatters to the floor when I try to carry
it from the kitchen to the chair.
The book dart falls into the folds of the blanket
as I attempt to mark the silky page that says,
Everything, everything becomes again.

Two weeks ago, I dreamed the Earth
was knocked off its axis, and an emergency alert
on our phones said, "No one knows now
what will happen." But we did know—
it was all going to fly apart.
And we waited, holding each other,
for it to happen.

Yesterday, the leaves dropped
from the maple in the warm wind
and took the orange light
from the white walls with them.

So it is into the cold blue I now stare
as I think how
we will need courage
and compassion
and hands
held together
like stars.

November 6, 2024

For Courage

When hate brews in neglected wounds
and collects like a darkening cloud
to roar down the throats
of the desperate,
let me take my fear in my hands
and mold it like dough.
Let me let grief rise in it
to meet the warmth of an unseen sun.
Let me bake it on the fire of love
to become bread to feed us with light
as we hunger in the shadow of the cloud.
And one of these lifetimes, let our light
grow out from the gray
and touch light.
I will meet you there.

Forgiveness

A wide corner bench
waits for you in an upstairs nook
with cherry wood rails
and warm, velvet cushions—
blue in the low lamplight.
A taper candle flickers on the table.
A window opens to the stars.

Would you sit here
and tell me which birds
fly over your skies?
And what world below
holds you
in its grip
and embrace?

I mean the you in your eyes
when they're wide—
the one who is small
and only as big
as the deepest love
you have known
and not known.

Maybe then, in the telling,
you might see how the night sky
and the softness and the flame
are not other
than your own self.
It is safe to love you.
It is safe.

Spirit Spiriting (Second Dog)

for L.

The cosmos
      shine out

from the large
      dark eyes

of this pleading
      little dog.

You know how it is
      with eyes.

Just when you think
      you know

what you are, you find
      yourself

another self
      deeper.

Stream over the Trail

Could I become the roundness
       of this water over these rocks
              smooth with millennia?

The kind of thing you hear running
       through trees from deep in a deep forest
              between high hills.

Fluid, small, something
       from the permanence
              that holds the impermanence

of flowing water, the erosion of rock,
       or the single drop of our presence.
              The cold silk slides across my sore feet.

Something in the bedrock of me knows
       where this water comes from
              and where it goes.

A Geode in a Dream

The rough crust of worn dust
that is the safety of my skin
cracks open.

Inside, a secret sea of purple,
a crystallized cloud of violets,
like breath took form
and shattered the morning air.

This is where I have kept the love
that now reaches in streaks
of light outward.

I keep nothing.
I lose nothing.

It is like remembering—
this dream of hidden
purple light like flame
reaching toward a whole host
of other shining flames.

To Time

It was You, wasn't it, on the mountain
when the wind stopped,

and my soul welled into the quiet
to roll with the peaks through the clouds?

When in the forest, I felt the earth
in my roots and the wind in my leaves?

You the tenderness in me for the finch
who no longer alights from the eave when I pass.

If all that exists matters, how does the river
carry on with calm assurance

when most days the smallness
of my understanding is my best hope?

I feel You unfold sometimes
like a purple flower after a rainstorm

as the pines drip spicy gold
into beams of old sunlight.

Then I want to love my way to You
straight through this body

and this sacred ground,
like a river.

To touch petals and plant seeds,
hold hands and scatter ashes.

I don't need to ask
if You'll have me.

Does the river ask the ocean
if it's ok to come home?

( )

Living and Dying

Beginnings turn to memories
I hold in the golden glow of evening.
When the first wisp of crisp air
once crossed the damp day with coolness.
Now the nights swelter, and November
is a state of being that permeates the whole calendar.
The foal in the near field trots to the fence
to nudge my hand with his velvet nose,
then frolics away to loll in a patch of sunlight.
An oriole flashes orange over the milkweed
into the gray hover of the trees.
A hand forever offers me itself, and I take it.
It is a time to kiss the ground
in the swell of this undoing.

In Harmony

When I wish
I could go back
from seeing,
I listen again
      to the trees
            sing with
                  the wind
until despair
rushes up
into longing
and the old fury hushes
      like a field of grass
            bows in waves
                of grief.
I breathe
the butterscotch wonder
of ponderosa pine
into my lungs until I know
      beneath my ribs
            what lasts and what matters
               have the same name.
In a dream,
I hear the song
in the wood of our walls
rise at dusk
      over the rooflines
            into the gold
               and purple clouds.

Gloria Patri in Snowflakes

for G.

The air is so cold
we hold form where we fell

on the ground the night before
and sparkle with the early sun.

The whole hillside
glitters.

We lock arms in our own
irreducible cold

with unnecessary
glory

the way beauty and pain
always live together.

Like grief and the sharing
of grief.

Or forgiveness
alongside hurt.

Soon we will sink into ourselves
and later, into the ground.

Our glory *in the beginning*
is now and ever.

In our ending worlds
a *world without end.*

Amen
Amen

I Try to Lay the Prayer of My Life
on the House of What Lasts

"… this is the other part of knowing something, when there
is no proof, but neither is there any way toward disbelief."
—Mary Oliver

Maybe it is the frigid wind
over the field where the coyote

ran in the night, or, as dusk descends,
the way the inside seems darker

than the outside's dark-tree, fence-line
silhouettes on the glowing snow.

The air is full
of something wild and good.

It is Christmas Eve.
I fly like the wind over each contour

of each print in the snow-tracked field
over the presence of this dog on my lap—

nearly constant these days
as his little body leaves him uncertain.

It raps on the door of his soul
until his feet twitch, trotting in sleep

like they've clicked at my side
down all the dark corridors of struggle.

He finds peace on my legs, so I sit
beneath his soft-breathing warmth

and learn to be this true,
this small, this entire.

It is my life's work
to know the shape of us—

what I can't, as this Oliver
also says, disbelieve.

We have no end.
It is inside out, like this light.

Notes

Epigraph
From "Tickets for a Prayer Wheel" Annie Dillard, *Tickets for a Prayer Wheel*, © 1974 by Annie Dillard. Wesleyan University Press edition. 2002. Used by permission.

"Ask Grief" [55]
Pierre Teilhard de Chardin, *The Divine Milieu*. Harper Collins Perennial Classics, 2001.

"Immersion" [60]
Karin Laub, "Cave Linked to John the Baptist," NBC News, August 16, 2004. www.nbcnews.com/id/wbna5724143

"Sassafras" [65]
Thanks to the Nature Center at McCormick's Creek State Park, Indiana, for the Get Sassy with Sassafras! program on October 8, 2022.

"Mo[u]rning" [78]
Cristina M. R. Norcross, "Everything Becomes Again," *The Poetry Apothecary*. Kelsay Books, 2024.

"*Gloria Patri* in Snowflakes" [88]
The *Gloria Patri* ("Glory Be to the Father") was sung as part of the liturgy every Sunday at the United Methodist church the author attended as a child. The lyrics are from the Lesser Doxology, 3rd to 4th century, fragments of which are italicized in the poem.

"I Try to Lay the Prayer of My Life on the House of What Lasts" [89]
Mary Oliver, "Bird," *Upstream*. Penguin Press, 2016.

Additional Thanks

The author would like to thank the following individuals whose time, generosity, expertise, and support made this collection possible:

Thirteenth-century Persian mystic Jalaluddin Rumi's zikr, as outlined by Coleman Barks in the footnotes of *The Essential Rumi* (Harper One, 2004), solidified the book's three-part form and expanded my reimagining of prayer in general.

Aaron Lelito provided early editorial guidance through *Wild Roof Journal*'s Individualized Poetry Manuscript Workshop.

Early readers Grace Bonewitz, B.A. Hollar, and Lisa Yoder helped focus the manuscript into its final stages with their careful consideration, feedback on core themes, and kind encouragement.

Ellis Elliott, Sarah Law, Aaron Lelito, and Nicholas Trandahl gifted the finished manuscript with their precious time and generous words.

Michelle Cochran helped pin down the right language for the book's description, based on her wisdom and experience in the Christian contemplative tradition.

Christine Brooks Cote of Shanti Arts gave this collection a home and put just the right finish on the book to make it what it is now.

The East Goshen Mennonite Church community received several of these poems in spoken form during worship with curiosity, grace, and loving support. Special thanks to attendees and participants of the tri-annual Poetry & Prayer group.

My parents, John and Dawn Wysong, believe in me as a writer more than I do.

Oliver warms my side through the countless hours of listening, reading, writing, revision, rethinking, and rewriting. Lewis reminds us to take breaks and stay limber with his pleading eyes and incessant flicking of the tennis ball at my legs. These two are my heart.

My husband, Mike, is steadfast in his support for me through the joys, triumphs, rejections, and disappointments of the writing journey. Thanks to him, the dogs, and the Earth, I know, as Rumi says, "the stronger pull of what I really love," and am drawn into Deeper Reality.

JENNA WYSONG FILBRUN lives in Indiana with her husband, Mike, and their dogs, Oliver and Lewis. Her poems have been nominated for The Pushcart Prize and Best of the Net and have appeared in a variety of literary magazines and journals. *Running Toward Water* is her second full-length collection of poems. She is also the author of *Away* (Finishing Line Press, 2023) and a chapbook, *The Unsaid Words* (Finishing Line Press, 2020).

Filbrun is currently a student in The Center for Action and Contemplation's Living School: The Essentials of Engaged Contemplation. She is a member of The Franciscan Action Network's Virtual Justice Circle and the Closer Than Breath online contemplative community. She attends East Goshen Mennonite Church and helps manage the tiny pantry at The Center for Healing & Hope. She works as an occasional math tutor and enjoys interacting with high school students and their families through her husband Mike's role as a high school math teacher and tennis coach.

Filbrun cares deeply for the Earth and the dignity of all beings. She and Mike enjoy hiking, especially in Colorado when they can make the trip west, watching episodes of *The Office* and random shows on PBS Passport, learning to identify nearby flora and fauna, and being out among the trees, plants, and creatures to listen.

SHANTI ARTS

NATURE • ART • SPIRIT

Please visit us online
to browse our entire book catalog,
including poetry collections and fiction,
books on travel, nature, healing, art,
photography, and more.

Also take a look at our highly regarded art
and literary journal, *Still Point Arts Quarterly*,
which may be downloaded for free.

www.shantiarts.com

www.ingramcontent.com/pod-product-compliance
Lightning Source LLC
Chambersburg PA
CBHW071354090426
42738CB00012B/3122